Rattlesnakes

Leo Statts

abdopublishing.com

Published by Abdo Zoom™, PO Box 398166, Minneapolis, Minnesota 55439. Copyright © 2017 by Abdo Consulting Group, Inc. International copyrights reserved in all countries. No part of this book may be reproduced in any form without written permission from the publisher. Abdo Zoom™ is a trademark and logo of Abdo Consulting Group, Inc.

Printed in the United States of America, North Mankato, Minnesota
062016
092016

 THIS BOOK CONTAINS RECYCLED MATERIALS

Cover Photo: Steve Byland/Shutterstock Images
Interior Photos: Shutterstock Images, 1, 6, 13; Ryan M. Bolton/Shutterstock Images, 4; Heiko Kiera/ Shutterstock Images, 5; Casey K. Bishop/Shutterstock Images, 7; Dennis W. Donohue/Shutterstock Images, 8; iStockphoto, 10–11; Red Line Editorial, 11, 20 (left), 20 (right), 21 (left), 21 (right); Norm Legault/Shutterstock Images, 12; Volt Collection/Shutterstock Images, 14; Rob Roeck/Shutterstock Images, 15; Bildagentur Zoonar GmbH/ Shutterstock Images, 17; Steve Byland/Shutterstock Images, 18–19

Editor: Brienna Rossiter
Series Designer: Madeline Berger
Art Direction: Dorothy Toth

Publisher's Cataloging-in-Publication Data
Names: Statts, Leo, author.
Title: Rattlesnakes / by Leo Statts.
Description: Minneapolis, MN : Abdo Zoom, [2017] | Series: Desert animals |
    Includes bibliographical references and index.
Identifiers: LCCN 2016941140 | ISBN 9781680791839 (lib. bdg.) |
    ISBN 9781680793512 (ebook) | ISBN 9781680794403 (Read-to-me ebook)
Subjects: LCSH: Rattlesnakes--Juvenile literature.
Classification: DDC 597.96--dc23
LC record available at http://lccn.loc.gov/2016941140

Table of Contents

Rattlesnakes

Rattlesnakes have a special tail.
Its tip is called a rattle.

They shake it when they sense danger.

Body

Rattlesnakes have big, pointed heads.

They do not have eyelids.
They sleep with their eyes open.

Rattlesnakes have scales.
Most are brown, yellow, or tan.
Their colors and patterns
help them hide.

Habitat

Rattlesnakes live in warm areas. Some live in North America. Others live in South America.

Where rattlesnakes live

You can find rattlesnakes
in **deserts** or forests.

They hide in holes
in rocks or logs.

Food

Rattlesnakes eat small animals. They eat mice and birds.

They eat lizards and rabbits, too.

Rattlesnakes bite their prey. Their fangs have venom. This kills the prey.

Life Cycle

Rattlesnakes have
live babies.

They shed their skin
each time they grow.

They live approximately
15 years.

Average Weight

A rattlesnake weighs more than a textbook.

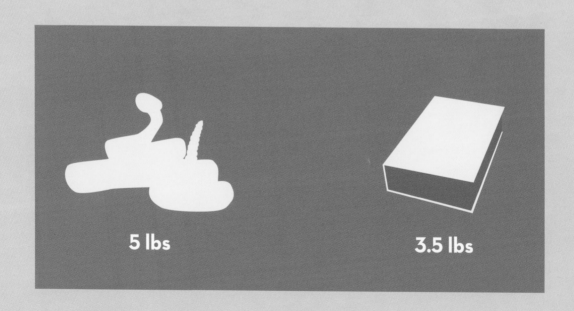

5 lbs

3.5 lbs

Average Length

A rattlesnake is roughly the same length as an acoustic guitar.

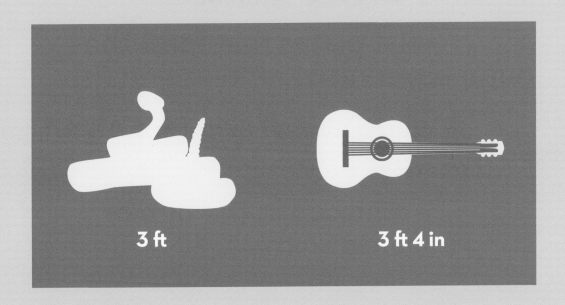

3 ft

3 ft 4 in

Glossary

desert - a very dry, sandy area with little plant growth.

fangs - long, narrow teeth.

prey - an animal that is hunted and eaten by another animal.

scales - flat plates that form the outer covering of reptiles and fish.

shed - when hair or skin falls off an animal's body.

venom - a poison in the bite or sting of some animals.

Booklinks

For more information
on **rattlesnakes**, please visit
booklinks.abdopublishing.com

 In on Animals!

Learn even more with the Abdo Zoom
Animals database. Check out
abdozoom.com for more information.

Index